LETTERS TO GUNS

March 2009

Matt,
Thank you for
your spirit &
generosity!

Letters to Guns

poems

Brendan Constantine

Blessings,
Brendan

RED HEN PRESS | *Los Angeles, California*

Book design by Sydney Nichols

ISBN: 978-1-59709-138-1
Library of Congress Catalog Card Number: 2008941042

The National Endowment for the Arts, the Los Angeles County Arts Commission, and the City of Los Angeles Department of Cultural Affairs partially support Red Hen Press.

Published by Red Hen Press
www.redhen.org
First Edition

ACKNOWLEDGEMENTS

The author gratefully acknowledges the publishers of chap books and periodicals in which some of these poems first appeared:

The Cider Press Review, "Aubade"; *Blue Arc West*, "Last Night I Went to the Map of the World and I have Messages for You"; *Ploughshares*, "Cold Reading"; *The Los Angeles Review*, "The Flickers"; *Beyond The Valley of the Contemporary Poets*, "The Golden Library of Knowledge...," The Day The Orchard Burned," "Apocrypha I," and "Kink"; *Abalone Moon*, "Meddling"; *Zombie Dovecote*, "One Million Years BC," "Gravelock," "Unsung Cheese," and "To Rain." All eight "Letters" first appeared in The Brickbat Review. Thanks are due also to both Mr. Donald Hall for his support of the poem "Unsung Cheese" and to Mr. Phil Van Tee for his support of "Gravelock."

Deepest thanks to: Cecilia Woloch for love and guidance in the wilds of poetry; to Suzanne Lummis and Laurel Ann Bogen for the first safaris; to Elena Karina Byrne for pointing and cheering; to David St. John for nodding and smiling; to Robert Wynne for raising the bar; to Nicole Harvey for painting the bar; to Rick Lupert for hiding the bar in the dark, dark jungle; to Mindy Nettifee for helping me find it again; to Arash Saedinia for not needing a bar or thanks; to Sarah Maclay for every last oyster; to Christopher Pitney for experience, strength, and hope; to Harvey Glass for explaining why I needed experience, strength, and hope; to Harriet Hall for the experience of her strength and hope; to Betsy Sholl, Richard Jackson, Clare Rossini, & Roger Weingarten for helping me come to the point; to Terrance Hayes & Mark Irwin for their generosity and art; to Tony de los Reyes and Anne Coates for their generosity in art; to Elizabeth Iannaci for the art of generosity; to Red Hen Press for taking a second look; to Carlye Archibeque for taking *The Wild Ones*; to Amelie Frank for wanting *The Pygmies* (all ten of them); to Scott Charles for making more pygmies; to Jeffrey McDaniel for believing in me regardless of my affiliation with pygmies; to Robert Arroyo for saying "Pygmies?"; to Jamie O'Halloran for reading to me over the sound of pygmies; oysters, guns, and leopard-skin talk; to Brigit Pegeen Kelly for the talk of the deer, the scorpion, and the trees; to my Aunt Mary Ellen for the tree-quiet love of a sister; to my sister and brother for the loud love of friends; to aunt Patty and Chris for faith & food; to Uncle Randy for laughter, loud or whispered; to Michael D for Irving Texas; to Nicole (Monk) for courage and more laughter; and to my Father and Mother for the world and the curiosity to address it.

Contents

PART III ~ STOPPING POWER

for Jayne

INTRODUCTION

It will come as a surprise to only 5% of Americans that the average, privately owned firearm receives approximately 4.6 letters a year. This is almost ten times that of any household appliance or national landmark. While half of these belong in the category of advertisements, this still works out to roughly 160 personal letters over a 70-year lifespan. The amount of correspondence for famous or noteworthy guns is considerably higher.

As the estimated number of Americans who read poetry is also 5%, I have sought to compile a brief history of this epistolary tradition and to do so in something like the manner in which it was revealed to me. Therefore the eight letters, which appear throughout this collection, are not presented chronologically but in their order of discovery. I have withheld signatures for obvious reasons.

It should be noted that the only other incorporeal addressee to receive more mail than the firearm is a statue of Confederate officer J. E. B. 'Jeb' Stuart in Richmond Virginia. Since its erection in 1907, the statue has received no less than 700 individual pieces of correspondence per annum. It has responded to every one.

Brendan Constantine
Los Angeles, California

PART I

BIG BANG

The greatest enemy of knowledge is not ignorance,
it is the illusion of knowledge.
—Stephen Hawking

ONE MILLION YEARS BC

The oceans were hot
and spat toothy fish into the air
like olive pits. Mountains
drooled fluorescent paint,
valleys filled with loose change
and lost sunglasses. In the jungles
great lizards walked on two feet,
carried flasks of warm lava,
and lied and lied and lied.
The trees had crude tattoos,
and dropped suitcases full
of money on the ground. Cats
with knives for teeth stalked
themselves under skies crowded
with sharp birds calling "Oh,
baby!" At night nothing walked,
the moon hissed at the ocean,
and the stars held each other
at gunpoint.

Letter IV

To an 1830 Henry Yellowboy 45
from a standard issue army boot
—Sharpsberg, Maryland, 1862

Dear Sir,

I embrace with pleasure this opportunity
to write to you, fitly as I can, of the last
day's events. Would that I could add
the observations of my twin, alas he is
no longer with me, but somewhere
on the bloody brow of South Mountain.
I know a prayer for him is leaving you
even as you read this.

I have been brought to the Antietam
Ironworks as yesterday our pickets
advanced this far to find the enemy
run off. I do not expect to be among those
in pursuit on account of my diminished state.
Neither do I wish to give in to hope
but if I understand what I have witnessed
of others similarly afflicted, I will soon be
worn to hospital or returned home.

I should note that as I write, it is evening
and the camp is besieged by a noise
as I have never before heard. There is a manner
of frog abundant in these parts given
to plighting its troth well unto dawn.
Some of the men complain of poor sleep
and palsied concentration. Indeed, I must
struggle to steady my pen as it tends to vibrate
with their withering songs.

My heart, though halved, hungers for news
of you, but I cannot say with certainty where
I will be in the time it takes for your response
to find me. It seems the essence of war
has become the burning of maps.
Perhaps it is best that you send word
home. Perhaps it will draw me there.

AUBADE

My love,
you have the right to remain
    silent. Anything you say
can and will be recorded
    in my pillow. If you desire,
you may request a transcript
    of every crushed feather.
You have that right, too.

Knowing
and understanding these
    rights as I sing them,
are you willing to answer
    without a moon present?
Put your hands in the air
    and walk toward me.
Tell me what you know.

COLD READING

It's really cold in here now,
easily forty below something,
and half the class is asleep.

Snow dazzles in the windows,
makes a cake of each desk.
It's really cold in here now.

I've been lecturing on the same
poem for twenty six hours
and half the class is asleep.

I want them to get it. I start
to talk about death again
and it's really cold in here now.

One student has frozen solid,
her hair snapping off in the wind
and half the class is asleep.

"See that" I say, "Lisa gets it."
But it's so cold in here now
half the class are white dunes
shifting to the sea.

And Abel

What my father didn't know
wouldn't fit into sky.
What my mother held back
wouldn't have helped.

My brother talked to dirt.

The truth was my family wasn't mine.
The truth was my sheep were smarter.
The truth was the snake bones
I often found in their dung.

My brother thought they were magic.

The day I died, we found a nest
of viper's eggs. My ram was still
eating the mother when the snakelets
broke their supple shells.

Some could not get out, the husks
bulged without breaking.
These I coaxed with a reed,
& set loose in the mud.

My brother had no idea

so I gave him one of mine;
I told him my skull was an egg, too,
the snake inside it helpless.
Then I turned from him,

walked slowly sunward.

Letter II

To a 'hand gonne' (first known handgun),
from a double handed broad sword
—London 1450 - 1490 ?

To hys worchepful master be thys delyvered in hayst

Black lamb, black bleat, thunder of the bullocks foete!
You are borne makeless ynd makeless you growe.
Cease you never now you are comme.
Cease you ever, No.

I am callyd Great Swerd, Great Swerd.
I Flourysh. I smyte. I stryke downryght
with a dragonys tayle. Double rownde
ynd double rownde then I stroke home.

Gaynward the sunne climeth ynd longe nightes
coureges dark, I sett my poynte
sofftley before you on the grownde.
I stoppe the morne you are comme.

White horse, wyde chase, melodye of the moony fayse!
I singe smalle werds fore you comme slowe.
But stoppe you never now you are comme
ynd I, Great Swerd, Great Swerd am go.

SLIDE SHOW

Here is her hand in Rome. Here
it is again on the Nile.

Here is her finger poised
over Stonehenge's

broken ring, as if deciding not
to wear it.

Your mother winks the world
through the hole

of her camera. She can't keep
clear of the lens

which is just below the view
finder. She thinks

they're the same. Some shots
are completely black.

Others are merely invaded a little,
like Paris.

This view of the city is flawless
but for its poked-out sun.

Look at Hawaii, its newest island
pink on the horizon.

The one of Buckingham Palace is
amazing;

your father and a palace guard
caught just before

being crushed by a wedding band.
Both appear to be
flinching slightly, bracing for it.
It could be the flash.

My favorites are the dark ones.
It's night

except in one corner. Here it's day
and there's water

or bricks or the shoe of someone
who waits to stop smiling.

When We Lived With The Bomb

We had a room in Queens with a couch that opened
into a second bed. I baby-sat odd nights, your father
worked from home, proof-reading phonebooks, some
days leaving only for cigarettes. One night I found
the two of them playing cards. *Look who I met
in line at the Larry's Liquor. And get this, it knows
my hometown.* Later it said the same thing to me
and I was from somewhere else. *Did you ever go
to the light house?* it asked. *Ever take a boat
on Misery Bay and wonder at the dead of 1812?*
We knew it wouldn't pay its way, clean house,
or feed itself. Maybe we needed the noise to hide
our silences. Maybe we needed a louder silence.
Anyway, we kept it—bought extra food, extra tickets.
If we went to the movies it sat between us, on the train
it stood and swung, if we fought it took no side but
stayed in the room. I recall thinking we should hide it
from the landlord, then watching with your father
when the landlord met it on the stairs, the way
it nodded confidently. *Do you know the old Belgrade
station? Do you remember the woman who sold
fortunes there? She told mine, too.* Eventually
we got better jobs, moved to the village. We said
it could stay on the couch, but it begged off, made
excuses about pride. It knew you were coming,
that you would cry, and how long.

MEDDLING

Before I wrote poems I meddled.
As a boy I would dress the dog
in my clothes and get my parents
to fight over who I resembled.
I told my brothers there was
no gravity and watched them flail
their short arms as they bounced
around the ceiling. Once I tore
a page from the kitchen calendar
and nothing happened for a month,
though I don't really remember it.
What turned me around was a night
in my eighteenth summer spent
watching old movies. I was tuning
our black & white when I touched
the glass and found it soft and wet.
Fitting my fingers into the frame
it came away in my hands like yolk.
The people in the film stopped
talking and looked around, startled.
I got ready for them to be angry
but instead they just stood there;
the man scratching his forehead
with the sight of his empty gun,
the woman smoothing her skirts,
unable to face me, my terrible colors.

THE DAY THE ORCHARD BURNED

The day the orchard burned was the first time
I heard Mozart. The entire crop was lost. I spent
sunrise at the feet of a dozen ladders while you
slept wherever you were sleeping then. The day
the fire chief "went up," I heard The Magic Flute
hummed end to end by a picker named Rudy.
The day the President passed out at the top
of a five iron shot, the day the dead plesiosaur
washed up on Hokkaido, I held a ladder
for a lunatic with a punctured hose and embers
catching in his beard and tried to save just one
peach tree. The day the televisions were recalled
for causing myopia, the day the virus shortened
the food chain, the day they found the Chinese
baby safe and fattened at the neighbors', I took
Mozart into my lungs and followed Rudy
until we both gagged like boot tongues; and all
around us ladders burned obscenely against trees;
and Chief Williams lost his way in his mask;
and the windshield blew out rhinestones
from the water truck. Rudy dragged behind me
like a piano, still humming between gasps, even
as he passed out on my shoulder. I took it up
and started again, finishing the prelude as we
flopped over the fence of somebody's house
and crawled to the swimming pool, a dog
barking in F Sharp from the diving board,
smoke playing over us in a wave.

APOCRYPHA

Poem to be read in private

You were born at the moment of war
between two constellations:
the Ten Armed Boy and the Two
Headed Girl.

Night by night you were told
a little more of what to expect
from your powerful blood. You
loved these stories.

Day by day the evidence grew
like the silver in your father's beard,
the orange stains
       in your mother's pot.

This morning of all mornings
you rise from perfect sleep
and go to the window.
Behold—

the prophecies were true, lustrous
with the first rub of sun,
the squirrel and grackle offer
themselves to you—

there is a note on your shimmering car!

Letter V

To a Coggswell and Harrison
double barrel elephant gun
from a grove of flame trees
—Kenya, 1954

Excellency

We refer this prayerful letter to You
with congratulations for the many loud noises
You have achieved in our humble country.
Blessings in the highest!

We are also comforted by Your concern
for our many large animals and desire
to rid us of their heaviness.

However, while not wishing to appear
ungrateful, we must ask that You leave
this problem to us. Tender willed traditionalists
we may be,

but we are unaccustomed to the task
of thriving without their burden.
If we are not sometimes food, we feed only ourselves.

Asking You, please, to accept the tribute of our colour,
with gratitude we will remain

STUDY

Panthera tigris

I'm painting a tiger, orange
for orange. There isn't much
black left to do—years, months,
God, hours may well be
involved—impossible to tell when

the ratio of ink to deer's blood is

a. as tender is to tendon
b. as game theory is to game trail
c. as museum is to stampede

Circle one,

one that looks sick or old.
Leave the calves, not enough meat
to fill a notebook. This is how
the tiger feeds the herd:

through its widest eye.

I say *Witness my hand & signature.*
Tiger says *Put your head in my mouth.*
        *Now try to speak. The jungle
        is like this, but all the time.*

Getting the tiger to be still is easy—
show him the painting so far.

Letting him move again requires despair.

INVOCATION OF THE SQUID

Note: the term Squid is alternately
high school slang meaning the same
thing as Square or Nerd, only more so.

O halfseen mover of the wounded
chair, before authors of Hit and Homework.
O sugar-pin guard of youth, wide
asleep in the anxious hall of Run
O eel killer of the public library
O fruit peeler
O stupid
O boy

O touch
O tentacle
O please not now

O now,
while coral fronds are eloquent
of paper fish and fortune tellers
while secret is your gasping note,
your portrait, your sticky oracle of Cut-
throat word and gesture, while blue
O wall-eyed arrow
O liar
O cheat
O frightened thief,
come by here
and be old.

PART II

RECOIL

If a blind man says, "Let's throw stones,"
be assured that he has stepped on one.
—Nigerian proverb

Letter VIII

To a 200 round box of Armor Piercing Incendiary Ammunition
from a Chevrolet Malibu abandoned at the corner of
15th Street and Columbia Road
—Washington DC, 2004

To Whom it may concern,

At 12:20 am on January 1st of this year, I received
a hole in my driver's side (and passenger) door
from an unknown sender. I believe I was sent this hole
in error. After consulting with other vehicles
in the neighborhood I have come to the conclusion
that it was likely delivered by one of you.

I am returning the hole herewith and demand,
in exchange, the purple hush of a morning
that should have been.

While I have no means to compel you, I trust
that your consideration of the enclosed vacuum
will induce you to avoid future complaints.

Allow them to gather and they will gather you.

And Only Once

Once,

when I was a girl, I watched a white swan
choke to death on my hairbrush
We were in a restaurant, the swan had
just ordered for me, a salad I think,
when he turned from the waiter, snatched
the brush from my hand, shook it
as if it were alive, as if it were dangerous
Then it was a shape in his throat
Then it was a trumpet full of sand
Then it was after midnight, a nurse
was saying something about a ride home
Once, when I was a girl, someone died for me
to be still

Twice,

when I was a girl, summer passed
in a single afternoon
The first time I was ten, harder to scare
so I remember little, but for the second
I was fourteen, nearly mad from being still
The entire season played out in front of me
like a rope tied to a rocket aimed at the sun
The next day, while yellow leaves dizzied
in my lap, I read of babies born with sunburns,
a train derailed by June Bugs   That year
my parents were carried off by sea gulls
Twice, when I was a girl, I drank a river of iced tea
and lived

Three times,

when I was a girl, someone told me I looked
too young to be wearing a rifle
Each time I sent them running for God
I read constantly then, anything I could get
my candied hands on

It didn't matter what language it was in,
if it had pictures of horses or the pages
fell apart as I turned them
My favorite book described the sadness
of the man who invented nitroglycerine
I knew I was meant to be him but he died
Every day that I was a girl, my hair caught fire
when I moved

Apocrypha

Poem to be read in private

Because the pines had deep voices
and the rocks none at all, the wild
dogs of the national park learned
to whistle. You could hear them,
or rather had you been a fox or rabbit
or some other steaming thing
born to be ripped apart you could have
heard them, whistling each other up
from miles away. They sounded
like screams and they sounded
like trains and they sounded
like bombs falling from aeroplanes.
Sometimes their songs were long
and continuous as if to accompany
the story of hunting you. But mostly
they were quick; a few notes
to say *You are close and I am*
close and together we are
one mouth swallowing God.
Each year some person or other,
a hunter or gatherer, would become
lost in the park and not be found.
They would confuse a rock or tree
for one they knew and lose
their way. As night came, they too
would hear the whistling, so like
the whistling of men, and mistake it
for someone come to find them.
They would follow or answer
with a whistle of their own
and well, you can imagine. Later,
when the dogs had finished them

and the bones or guns of the lost
people lay drying, the pines might
say something low and a rock or two
might whisper, but nothing memorable.
Nothing that stayed in the ear.

The Need to Leave

a dog is barking
a woman is sleeping
a man is old

the world of this world
is what it is doing
everything else is night

a candle is finding a road
a long coat is wearing
a boy is worn

one shoe is untied
two buttons are missing
five coins are a bowl of soup

but a village is ferocious
the hours of this hour
will not intervene

a cow is eating
a barn is sulking
a window is burning out

someone is coming
an open door is an open door
a mouse is gone

a knife, a bag of clothes,
a photograph of a horse
the need of this need

travels with us

MEETING THE AUTHORS

I'm talking to the children about strangers.
They're people your parents haven't met,
I say, *They're everywhere.* Now I want
to know what the children know.

What does a stranger look like?

It's a man, they say — my fault, perhaps,
I've been saying *He* all day. But like mice
they have gathered bright things
from who knows where.

He's tall, has a beard, brown eyes

with gold flecks, a long coat. His pockets
are full of candy & broken glass. He has
toys which he makes himself, or inherits
from the children who speak to him.

If you go with him, he will keep you.

The stranger has no name — no name.
You don't call him. You draw him out
by being alone or not looking
at clocks, by making up
              what you haven't been told.

THE MISSING

As far as I can tell, they've stopped
putting the faces of lost children
on milk cartons. The brand I buy
used to devote a whole panel
to them with the words
Have you seen these children?
Ha visto usted estos niños?
in the same red ink as the image
of the smiling cow on the label.
I want to ask the cow if she's found
them. It's pleasing to imagine
this, if only for a moment; the children,
thousands of them, standing
in a red field beneath a red sun
holding hands or stroking
her glossy coat.

The cigarettes I smoke are packaged
with a single trading card depicting
an endangered animal: the Mandrill,
the Ocelot, the Green Sea Turtle;
each of them realized in full color.
I've been saving them, a pack
at a time, in a small tin box shaped
like a car. It's all I can do. Today
I found a Black Footed Ferret, perched
on a snowy slope in Wyoming.
He looks back at me now from
the top of the deck, his masked
head tilted slightly, searching
for the photographer whose scent
has stopped his hunting.

LETTER VI

To a Walther PPK from the inside pocket of a men's wool sport jacket
—East Berlin, Germany, 1963, translated in part by a Univac III
Solid State Computer employed by the Central Intelligence Agency

Leibshin,

Desperate the hours that I for word
of you wait are. Your quiet a desolateness
like the sky is. So complete alone I am
if you not with me are, that even in a room
that full of people is, I am a planetary
orphan morsel to cough the milk of space.
This hiding ugly is. Where you are?
Where you are? To me please write
that you home are coming, and will again
inside me be.

Inside me be,

LAST NIGHT I WENT TO THE MAP OF THE WORLD
AND I HAVE MESSAGES FOR YOU

America says it has misplaced your number.
I wasn't comfortable giving it out. I said
I'd let you know.

Africa's birthday is this weekend.
There's a party. No gifts.
                              Just come.

If you're planning to go, Greece wants
to know if it can get a lift. Awkwardly
                              so does Turkey.

Russia wanted me to say *The worm knows
the cabbage but the worm dies first.*
I have no idea what that means. Do you?

Japan looked really uncomfortable all night
but never spoke. Is something going on?

Ireland asked to be remembered.
I sang to it for you.

I didn't get to connect with Europe
but, as the French say, *Isn't that just
                              too bad.*

Is that everyone? Oh yes, the oceans.
They asked what they always ask
and I promised I'd repeat it,
                    Why do you never call?
                       When are you coming home?

GRAVELOCK

11 bumper stickers for coffins, after Phil Van Tee

I was randomly kind
and senselessly beautiful

I loved my dog

I loved my kids

I loved New York

I am the proud parent of a million ants

My other car is the wind

My other car is a field of asphodels

This is my other car

Don't laugh, it's paid for

Don't laugh, I'm ahead of you

Laugh all you want

KINK

A recent survey of fetishes has named
feet & shoes the world's greatest objects
of desire. Perhaps surprisingly, lingerie trails
at some distance. Further behind, less than
four percent, are genitals, breasts, buttocks
& legs. They appear, as they often do,
in a pile at the end of a line. The only token
of longing more remote is the electric
pacemaker, for which two people indicated
strong attractions. Much is being made
of the champions, pedicure & shoe sales
have soared, but who can stop thinking
about the losers? The study comes from Italy,
a country formed like a sultan's boot,
but its range is global; no one knows where
the two people live, if they've met, or how
they love. Most of us must see a thing to know
we need it. Even the blind learn shapes
of yearning. A pacemaker is small as a kiss
& works quietly in the dark of the body.
Working at what? The constant arousal
of slow hearts with beats of lightning,
like snapping fingers, like a whip. Maybe
the two lovers are doctor & nurse, or a pair
of electricians. Perhaps they're mad, people
so crazed with loneliness, so at the mercy
of blood, the mere thought of its mastery is
rapture enough. Anyway, now there are three.

SHROUD

Ambrose Bierce said all reports of ghosts
wearing shrouds were unreliable. Whatever
powers of apparition might bless the flesh
could hardly be expected of cotton, silk,
or wool, otherwise we ought to see
old clothes appearing on their own
from time to time. I once called the home
of a dead man to offer sympathy to his wife.
A machine with the man's voice answered
& told me to leave a message, he'd try
to call back. Somehow I could tell
he was wearing a robe over bed clothes.
I could hear his thick socks, the Kleenex
in one pocket, a pillbox. The first shrouds
were blankets, then ropes on boats. Now
they're the skins of spaceships, allowing
them to leave the earth & return cool
as night birds. The cries of whippoorwills
sound like mourning. At sunset, they fly
over the bay, an arrow of empty shirts.

A History of Sympathetic Navigation

an annotated poem

Long before we[1] agreed on the time
in Greenwich, a group of velveteen men
was charged with finding[2] longitude at sea.
They feared[3] unless the Atlantic could be
accurately mapped, it[4] would become so full
of sunken ships, the French might one day
walk across to wherever they[5] pleased.
Priests and mathematicians were called
to advise and Sir Isaac Newton[6] proposed
a machine. The answer turned up
on a hill, 170 years[7] away. But of all
the bad ideas[8] in that time[9], there is one
champion bad idea[10] that continues to pace
its kennel in history[11]. It employed a remedy
know as The Powder of Sympathy[12], a talc
that could torture[13] or soothe the wounds
of soldiers when applied to the weapons
that scarred[14] them. Every ship would be given
a dog wounded[15] by the same knife, a knife
kept in London. At noon a man[16], trained
for the job[17], would thrust[18] the blade
into The Powder of Sympathy[19], inducing
the dogs at sea to cry out. Thus the captain
would know it was twelve[20] back[21] home.
There's no record of a test dog or journey,
no credit[22] remains for the authors[23]. Only
a log book of *also rans* and the fact[24]
of no weeping dogs on airplanes[25].

1 And now I must enter the poem
2 so that you know how to reach me.
3 Once you've heard such a thing
4 it stays close, like a lost animal.
5 Months afterward I could hear them.
6 I had to learn how to fall
7 asleep to the howling, to heavy clocks.
8 That's where the trouble always starts,
9 isn't it?
10 Knowing too much?
11 It doesn't matter that it didn't happen,
12 the idea belongs to you now.
13 Your head is filling with ships, bestormed
14 on account of a dog who cried noon
15 all day. In the mornings
16 your hands may smell like rope,
17 it may take a while to get your balance.
18 Things will get worse for a bit
19 when you remember the men,
20 when you make faces for them.
21 They'll start showing up
22 dressed as businessmen or cops;
23 sometimes they're even children.
24 I'll be here if you need me
25 to talk you down.

The Flickers

Not for their hard lace have I tried
to write of them forever now, though
it's reason enough, the patterns of holes
they make in our eaves, so like lace, some
people don't repair them. My neighbor
swore the birds had deliberately carved
flowers or faces into his shutters, swore
so loud it shortened his life. But a pale man
from the college heard him, studied the holes,
& declared them proof art was genetic.
I still don't know what to do with that,
as I say, it isn't my reason for wanting
words. Neither is it because the flickers
do this only on the sunward sides
of houses or how they sort their acorns
into the holes as if to punctuate some
& not others. Once they've finished,
they go. What haunts me like creaking,
like the voice of wood, is what happens
when they come back after the acorns
have cooked for a few days. They listen,
they listen to the acorns, they cock
their heads like old men on porches
& listen for the hot playing of a worm.
If they hear nothing, they knock. Tell me
it's enough to say this. Whoever you are
out there, tell me I don't need to go on
about the trail of holes I've left, the buried
books & boxes, the hands of lovers held
to my ears that I might catch a whisper
of something like *Come in.*

PART III

STOPPING POWER

*But while our mouths have spittle in them
the whole country is still armed.*
—Marina Tsvetaeva

SHORT CUT

You go down here
for a little way until you come to
a sign, something red and quick.
Then you turn and go straight
for a spell.

When you get to the ducks
keep going. You'll see a bunch
of houses with people standing
out in front. Some of them will
have sad faces

or will be crying.
Don't stop. It's nothing you did.
Just head for the cemetery. Five
or six graves in there's a statue
of Clio, the muse of history.

Look where she's pointing.

Unsung Cheese

after Donald Hall

In the central library the epic poems of cheese starve for
themselves while unnamed cheeses lose their histories entirely;
Feta gone to pieces like the Parthenon; Mozzarella, foreign
gentleman graciously contained until spoken to.

O cheeses of legend, cheeses of Nazareth, cheeses that pray
openly in public because everywhere is God. O cheeses
of the forests and streams, cheeses of industry, cheeses
that turn with the gears of commerce, making and breaking.

American cheese, youngest of contenders, selling out
until the world is yours; Monterey Jack, notorious
waterfront thug; Gouda, temptress and geometrix,
modeling nude for businessmen and mathematicians.

O cheeses of poverty, cheeses of social security, cheeses
crippled and couch-ridden before the television, losing
the remote control between thyroidal cushions. Nacho cheese,
addicted to everything, waiting for the telephone to ring.

Cheese Wiz, fluorescent pimp, hustler, and teenage prostitute,
buying beer with a fake ID; Provolone, fixing a horse race
for La Cosa Nostra; Asiago, taking a fall in the first round;
and Fontina, Prince of Denmark, your days are numbered.

O forgotten cheeses of war, cheeses that cram the orphanage,
vandalizing churches, looting summer homes, always disappearing
in the night, your pockets heavy. O cheeses of the single-parenthousehold,
cheeses suspicious of authority.

Gloucester, whispering the fall of the monarchy; Havarti
fickle romantic, ruining the wedding with your indifference;
Parmigiano, playful but easily alarmed; and Romano,
leaving your lovers early to call mother long distance.

O stories of cheeses, I memorize you for my unborn children.
O cinema of cheeses, revived at midnight in university towns,
O cheeses that languish in books like the lyrics of lost empires,
this mercy, this forgiveness, these hands describing love.

LETTER VII

To a Taurus Model .38 Special
from a woman's flannel night-gown
—San Bernardino, California, 1999

You stupid bastard,

What the hell am I supposed to do now?
There might be enough cold water
in the world to flood the stain,
but who is gonna close this hole?
Her kids? They're so freaked out
they don't recognize their names.
And dad is as drunk as a mudslide.
Incidentally, he's telling the cops
he doesn't know you. Do me a favor,
find his fucking hand again.

THE TWO BLIND MEN
AT THE JACOB EPSTEIN EXHIBIT

made a lot of noise coming in
stayed close to the docent
walked through us like firemen
wore shirts half tucked
wore white gloves to touch the sculptures
touched the sculptures
went straight for the middle each time:
>Paul Robeson's nose
>Albert Einstein's nose
>the belly of a sleepwalking woman
>the plexus of a warrior
>the brief cleft between two mounting doves
>the missing sex of an angel

worked their way out
laughed a lot
cried once
asked to come back tomorrow
said Thank You
ordered a taxi
made fun of the deaf going out

POSTMORTEM OF PRESIDENT ABRAHAM LINCOLN
AS OBSERVED BY A PASSING TRAWLER

As the streets flooded, and the stars tacked over them, so
        the country set adrift on Mr. Lincoln's face.
    An aid riding with the martyred president, observed
    sea water pouring from the back of his head. "I recall
    the carriage suffused with perfumes of the Atlantic.
    I then sensed a coldness by my ankle and discovered
    several small fish had loosed from my president's vest
    to gasp about the floor."
By the time it had reached the White House, the hearse had to
        be cleared of a multitude of bright shells
    before the body was removed. Attempts were made
    to occupy the First Lady by holding an empty nautilus
    to the storm of her ear, that she might calm and permit
    herself to be borne away.
She would not be removed from her husband's side nor distracted
        from her peculiar prayers for his soul, "I hear
    the fair color of my Lord's gown of glory. It shadows me
    from sorrow, it shines me with His love. . ."
On relinquishing him to his many doctors, she was observed
        to faint upon a bed of squid outside the East Room.
    Thus startled the creatures but briefly emulated the colors
    of her gown, and then again became the floor.
    Assistant autopsy surgeon Edward Curtis was put in charge
    of recovering the bullet and any Spanish doubloons
    which may have materialized in the geocentric tumult
    of the president's unmaking, these last to be applied
    to the costs of committing his remains to the earth.
Sovereigns were not found in the president's brain, though
        Curtis wrote in his log, "Suddenly the bullet
    dropped out through my fingers and fell, breaking
    the solemn silence of the room with its clatter.
    There it lay upon the white china, a little black mass

no bigger than a mackerel's eye, yet the cause of such
mighty changes in the world as we may never realize."

Japan upon Egypt China crashing into Dover! The fatter the moon,
　　　　　　the hungrier the tide. How the ground shook, how
the towers swayed, how the gravediggers plighted. No sooner
had the president's coffin been set in the ground, than it began
to bury itself beneath gluts of sand squalling from it's seams.
Blessings were invaded by gulls who attacked mourners
and polluted the eulogy with their cries.
Mrs. Lincoln endeavored to sing in their manner, but they heeded not
　　　　　　her hymns, if that was what they were.
　　　　Prayer, like all music is a thing described only
　　　　by more of itself.
I, who was not there and know what I saw, who calls attention
　　　　　　to himself only now the bereaved are all below,
　　　　I am just a swell, a trawler, a Jonah not welcome in church
　　　　or before the mast. Nor will I ever be
　　　　if I keep breaking my lines. God ignores poets,
　　　　　　but only in public; at night He casts us fathoms of rope.
Solvitur Ambulando　　*It is solved by walking*, so saith the statues
　　　　　　in the park. They pose, they posture,
　　　　but dare not wave as I pass, sorting out the starfish
　　　　from the stars, the assassins from the actors,
　　　　the faces of great men from their cold coins.

THE NEED TO STAY

My mother says there is only one philosophical
question that needs answering:
                    Are you staying or going?

She says a Frenchman said it first but who's
counting? He's dead.

Ten, nine, eight . . .

There are no prime numbers. Just small actors.
We are all divisable. Going means no more questions.
                    Are you staying?
If so, Happy Birthday.

Seven, five, three . . .

My father knew a man who died of a bee sting.
Was he allergic? I asked.
                    No, he said, *A tightrope walker.*
My father says it was murder.

Two, two, two . . .

He says there are men in Toulon who train bees
to count and act in films. They cannot, however,
teach them to fall. Or rather, not more than once.

One . . .

Today I met a Funambulist. Been walking wires
since he could walk. We were in a garden on his roof
and he told me there are days

                   when the ground calls to him.

What's it say?

Stay.

THERE

We're bad wicked teachers. We're going
to hell. The children prepare us all day.
One boy with a skinned knee says
it's like two skinned knees, and always.
For the girl on a swing, it's her mother's
attention. It hurts, *ucky-icky-mean*. Ask
anyone in the park; it's a swallow of earth,
a cherry stone open in the belly, a tree
that grows from your mouth, then back
into the ground. We'll spend the sky
that way, our backs bent, our apologies
stifled like yawns.

VARIATIONS ON A THEME
BY FERDINAND MAGELLAN

This is everything.
  This is all we can carry.
    This should be the last of it.
    Run upstairs and check.
I just want to have one more
  look around. Once more
    around the city wall.
      The village is deserted.
        The apartment is empty.
          The house is locked up.
            We've poisoned the well.
          The neighbors have keys.
        The dogs will take care of things.
We're bringing the dogs with us.
  The tent should be fine.
    No one will find the cave.
      No one else is coming.
        A lot more people are coming.
          Dad's coming.
            Mom's ready.
              Your sister
          should be right down.
      I don't know what's keeping
your brother. The men are assembled.
      We're leaving the women.

      I'll meet you outside.
        I'll wait in the car.
          I'll wait with the others.
            We should wait for everyone.
              We should wait for the wind to pick up.
            Wait for the rain to stop.
Wait for fresh horses.

The horses know the way.
　The ship is an old one.
　　It's one of those huge planes.
　　　The train is like when we were kids.
　　　　There are sandwiches and everything.
　　　　　There's barely enough food.
　　　　　Bring only water.
　　　　　Anything we forget,
　　　　　　we can buy.
　　　　It should be pretty full.
　　　We're lucky to get seats.
　　We ought to have
　　the whole thing
　　to ourselves.
　　　　The tickets are in my coat.
　　　　　The tickets are in your purse.
　　　　　　We'll pick up the tickets there.
　　　　　The instructions say Midnight.
　　　　They say *NO COPS*.
　　　　The invitation is for one.
　　　It's just you and a friend.
There are 200 crew.

　　We have digital charts.
　We have Portuguese maps.
　We have a dash-board Buddha
　　with a compass in his belly.
　　　There are signs we can follow.
　　　Big arrows. Bright stars.
　　　The moon. It's all lit up.
　　　You can't miss it.
　　　　There should be a big crowd.
　　　　A line 'round the block.

Look for a mountain.
Look for a pile of rocks.
Look for the words
YOU ARE HERE.

And here the directions end.
Here the page runs out.
Here the road just stops.
The horses spook.
The wings fall off.
The river flows back
to the jungle. Here,
take the wheel.

LETTER III

To a .69 cal. Charleville Musket from a wooden spoon
—Arles France, 1790

Mon Cher President

I am desolated to write you
with no address but the past.
Do you remember our last meeting?
We watched from a summer table
as the sun cooked our harvest
in the ground, fed it to the sky.
You asked what I was thinking
and I said I had discovered my own
uselessness. *Write it down*, you said.

The master carried you away shouting,
carried you to war. To my shame, I hid
in a drawer. I come out this morning
having filled a calendar with writing.
I see it was not impotence.
It is my own revolution.
Can anything be more natural?
Breath is revolution, sleep and waking.
War is a season of the body with songs.

There are always songs, no?
All rebellions the same: once they start
no one can remember why or agree
how they should end. Music is a child
of such uncertainly. Who sings in Eden?
A bird of paradise is a flower, not a bird.
I leave my songs to the dark. The only
cause of the servant is service.
I am coming to serve you.

Do you sing? What do you sing?
I've found a six month letter from you
sent from nowhere. Why open it
when it may no longer be truth.
Do you still shout? Still say God
is a blacksmith? Say He will not
forsake the handy?
I am coming.

My family is with me but none dare
speak of you. We are set out for supper
in the same summer kitchen. I alone
am missing you. The others are too
amazed by death, for the sun still
prowls our fields. They do not see
it is only beautiful, but you would, no?
Death for us is to live unused.
I am coming.

How French it is to know the heart
is talked out of nothing. How absurd
that it is only threatened by beauty.
Arm yourself for beauty. Shout at it,
sing that I am coming. Over war
and music, in God's blackened teeth
I am coming.

THE BOUNTIFUL

The ripe ripe wounds of the chest, that give & give, look
& look. Wounds that are like eyes, eyes too full of paintings
of wounds, bigger than the eyes of a girl, of a man, of a whale;
fish shaped wounds; starfish-exit wounds; Natural-History-
Museum-entry wounds, her coat caught in the heavy heavy door,
his sleeve caught in the elevator, his wife caught a glimpse
on their honeymoon, they did not speak of it.

Wounds that fit in the mouth - peach, plum, and tomato;
the sour wounds of the leg; the intelligent wounds of the arm,
the many many many wounds of the hand, wood cut, paper cut,
sugar cut. Wounds of the lower spine, said by swordsmen to be
sweet, delicious; wounds on the cheeks of German swordsmen,
the *Schmiss*, an award from the master, a trophy for skill
with swords, with choosing wounds for other swordsmen.

Wounds wounding the already wounded. Wounds that are full
of wine, full of sand, or ash; wounds of remarkable men; Shhh!
Women's wounds, of the womb, the hip, the heel. The most royal
wounds of the neck; wounds hidden by the glove or telephone,
by the scarf or collar; collars of leather, chain, or ermine, below
gold & velvet crowns. The bountiful wounds of the head.

Wounds that laugh, so easily laugh at the icicle, the skillet,
the hammer, found in the woods behind the house, ruby cross
almost lost in the sphagnum. Open wounds; closing wounds;
casual wounds, Sicilian necktie, Christian Crown, Poet's Bracelet;
wounds that complete majesty, begin eternally, the eternal wounds
of the lips. Wounds that fit in the mouth, to be drawn,
to be coaxed to speak.

THE WILDFLOWERS

Last night my love brought me wildflowers
and as we lay together in the easy dark
I heard them leave the vase, and move
around the house. When I woke, my love
was gone,
        the flowers watched me walk
from room to room. They followed me
with a wet-dry sweep and shuffle that was
something like my own breath, never close
never within reach.
        I couldn't get near them,
they curled if I faced them or turned out
their clear barbs to warn me off.
        Now
they are drinking at the sink. The light
begins to rust on the sill and I know,
as I watch them push each other
out of the stream, they are preparing
for night's second ceremony, the hunt.

"THE GOLDEN LIBRARY OF KNOWLEDGE
IS A SERIES OF BOOKS ESPECIALLY DESIGNED
FOR TODAY'S GENERATION OF YOUNG PEOPLE
EAGER FOR INTERESTING AND FACTUAL KNOWLEDGE"

Carefully researched and authoritative
Carefully written to be easily read
Carefully considered by careful people
Carefully careful
Careful attention is paid to detail,
to colors, to lines, to the habits of animals
Carefully the lion takes position in the grass
Careful to make no sound
It kills carefully, you know
Carefully the zebra, carefully the deer
Carefully the hunters crawl on their bellies
Carefully researched and authoritative
like scientists, like criminals, like books
The Planets, The Sea, Butterflies & Moths,
The Fighting Indians of the Old West
careful to make no sound
Carefully careful
So careful they are gone
If you are careful you can still find one
I found a Navajo and he told me
If you are not swift be careful
If your are not clever be careful
If you are not greedy, be very careful
Be careful of men
Be careful of animals
Be careful of what you read
or you may be written upon
and kept forever in a Golden Library of Knowledge
and cared for, terribly cared for
by careful people

by mathematicians
by the great philosophers
by the slave-making ants of the Amazon
So careful they are gone
Gone to waste in books
to wait in museums
to recombine in genetic swamps
to colors, to lines, to the habits of animals
Today's generation of young people
carefully forgetting yesterday's generation
of careful old people
Carefully researched and authoritative
Carefully careful
Careful in their sleep
Carefully knitting up the ravelled sleeve of care
It kills carefully, you know
The animal that kills you
The book that kills you
The interesting fact
that no matter how careful you are
you may be written upon
Carefully written to be easily read
and cared for, terribly cared for
like scientists, like criminals,
The Fighting Indians of the Old West,
The Greeks and the Amazons
fighting still in the radio libraries of space
The Planets, The Sea, Butterflies & Moths,
Carefully recumbent in the genes
Carefully expressed in color and line
Carefully absorbed in the mind by the eye
Carefully drawn in the mouth by the tongue
Carefully scattered in the blood by the stomach
where care is born, where it is broken down.

ERRATA

The smile your father saw in the wallpaper
had nothing to do with your mother. There
were dozens of faces in the flowers, had he
taken the time to look. Many of them were
weeping, buckets of wisteria. Still he was
right to ask for her hand. The scorched
curtain that sent him away five years later,
however, was right on the money. It meant
Take the children. She'd have burned you
in her sleep.

        Your grandfather would still be
alive if he hadn't trusted the gulls. They were
lost when they passed over his boat, nowhere
near land. Your grandmother's vision that night
—the ship's cat soaking wet at the foot of her
bed—well. . .that was a kind of grace little seen
anymore.

        Indeed, a deep breath has been cut
from this evening in error. Put it back. It comes
when you step from the shower. You need
a moment to see the mirror; the veins of steam
forming a shape beneath your reflection. Let it
remind you of a word & go to bed. Ignore
those patterns in the ceiling. No good
can come of them.

Apocrypha

Poem to be read in private

Once, before guns,
         a jobless assassin walked
through the marketplace with his hands
in his unlikely pockets, letting his eyes
linger only on red things: meat, blankets,
a monkey.

         He'd had no work
for a season, could see none coming—
no drought, no election, not even a wedding
anniversary—not one symptom within
his cure.

         At the end of the square
he turned and sought the oldest merchant.
Whispering in the man's dry ear, he said
You were right about him all along.
Look for me tomorrow.

LETTER I

To a pot of huo yao,
(original formula for gunpowder)
from a pot of ink
—China, Han Dynasty, 206 BC - 219 AD

Happy Birthday Cousin

The ground shakes, the sky delights
at your first cries. How you keep us awake!
From this time forward you will summon
the new year and shout away the old.
Bright lotus of winter, wayward star,
you will do little else until you are grown.

I write to you with tidings of luck
and warnings of fortune. Like you
I began life as something only beautiful;
a permanent bloom, a word for spring.
By the time twelve moons had passed
I knew each color in the eye.

Then I was spilled, ran everywhere,
the land was stained with language.
It was not carelessness, but destiny.
I play my memories like a harp song;
with each recital, I learn again the folly
of regret in the echo of time.

The day you are spilled, the earth
will be poisoned, but do not be troubled.
It will learn to swallow you as it did
blood, as it did me. It learns all rivers,
though you will not stay a river.
Your fortune is rain. War.

A sword is an oar to paddle through men
but it wearies the traveler quickly.
The warrior who wields you will pass
through an army like sunlight
through the sweet tea he drinks
in his enemy's garden.

You will know many glories, your strength
last many centuries. Though I am already
old, I will go where you go. I will write you
a thousand names. You will speak only one.
Twins but not brothers, cousins but not clan,
we will die on the same day.

NOTES

"Letter I": The Chinese term *hue yau* literally means "fire drug" or "fire medicine."

"Letter II": The words "flourysh," "smyte," "chase," and "dragonys tayle" are all authentic terms for movements of the broad sword.

"A History of Sympathetic Navigation": The Powder of Sympathy was a real remedy and it's proposed use as described in the poem was put before the Board of Longitude as a legitimate tool for navigation. We do not know if it was tested. We do know it was not adopted.

"The Golden Library of Knowledge . . .": Takes its complete title from the jacket notes in a series of Natural History books for children.

The quote which begins part three is taken from poem six of Marina Tsvetaeva's "Poems To Czechoslovakia."

Biographical Note

Brendan Constantine is a poet based in Los Angeles. He holds a masters degree from Vermont College of Fine Arts and his work has appeared in numerous journals, most notably *Ploughshares, The Los Angeles Review, The Cortland Review, The Cider Press, RUNES,* and the LA Times bestseller *The Underground Guide To Los Angeles.* He is the creator of Industrial Poetry, a workshop for adults and teens struggling with writer's block. He teaches poetry at both the Windward School in West Los Angeles and the Idyllwild Arts Summer Youth Writing program in Idyllwild, California. He lives in Hollywood at Bela Lugosi's last address.